Service-Oriented Security Primer for Managers

Ola Osunkoya, Ph.D

978-0-6151-9410-3

@Copyright 2008

It is illegal to reproduce any part of this book without the written permission of the author

E-infoseckonsult publishing

109 Pine Cone court

Cedar brook, NJ 08081

Acknowledgement

This book is dedicated to my God who is the head of my life and has spared me through his grace to see this day even in my polluted blood, my loving wife, Olufunke Osunkoya, who never gave up on me when I was acting a fool, who always have a word of encouragement when I'm feeling weary, who goes to war with me despite all the odds that may be against us, my daughter, Tomisin Osunkoya, who has taught me patience and has given me a reason and a purpose for fatherhood and to my spiritual parents, Dr. Lamont Mclean and Pastor Connie Mclean with the five Ministers of Living Faith Christian Center, NJ who through their obedience to teach and live the Word of God, I have been able to raise up a Godly family by following their faith.

109 Pine cone court

Cedar brook, NJ 08081

@ 2007 by e-infoseckonsult

Table of Content

Chapter 1 4

    Background 4

    What is Service-oriented architecture? 6

    Why businesses welcome this development 9

Chapter2.. 12

    State of problem.. 12

    Existing Security model 15

    Issues with using perimeter model to secure SOA.................................... 15

    Architecture and Implementation requirements for SOA security................. 17

    Service-oriented security architecture overview................................... 24

    Service-oriented security views... 26

    Service-oriented security models, standards and mechanisms.................... 33

    Service-oriented security management... 38

    Service-oriented security issues... 40

Chapter 3 42

    How the research contributes to the security industry body of knowledge........42

    Future trends in SOA security... 43

Chapter 4 44

Chapter 1

I. Background

The increasing pace of the evolution of business requirements and the need for increased revenue and cost optimization are leading corporate executives to deliberately align their information technology organizations more closely with their business requirements. The main goal of this convergence is to develop more optimal and operationally integrated business processes that can be implemented by departments, business units and business partner networks. Historically, the convergence process has been constrained because information technology systems have not kept in step with business needs and the infrastructure has inherent operational and developmental limitations, such as proprietary programming interfaces that restrict a system's flexibility. Consequently, the integration challenge demands a technology that can successfully bring together the needs of business and IT into a viable solution that not only makes efficient and effective use of the infrastructure, but also flexible and adaptive enough to keep pace with continual changes in the organization's business process and business models.

The concept of service-oriented architecture (SOA), offers a framework for better integrated systems that meets business needs. SOA envisions the implementation of a service platform consisting of many services that signify element of business processes that can be combined and recombined into different solutions and scenarios, as determined by business need. The capability to integrate and recombine services is what provides the closer relationship between business and IT, as well as the flexibility to address new situations.

The role of SOA service platform is to provide a foundation for delivering essential business services in a flexible, easily composed and highly reusable fashion. From a business point of view, a SOA can be expressed as a set of flexible services and processes that a business wants to expose to its customers, partners, or internally to other parts of the organization. In this context, the same services can be recombined and supplemented to support changes to or an evolution of business requirement and models over time. From a technical point of view, SOA defines software in terms of discrete services, which are implemented using components that can be called upon to perform a specified operation for a specific business task. The SOA concept evolves the existing software concept of a function (a specific piece of code that performs a particular task), to include the notion of a contract (a technology-neutral but business-specific representation of the function). This notion evokes similarities to component orientation which is another software development approach that also promotes the idea of constructing applications from the assembly of reusable building blocks called components.

II. What is Service-Oriented Architecture

A real world analogy will help describe and define Service-oriented architecture. In general, each person has a particular capability. However, there is not necessarily a one-to-one mapping between his needs and capabilities. For example, if I wanted to build a house and I have a piece of land and adequate financing, but not the necessary expertise to build a good house. This means that I need to consult an architect for a home plan. In this case, there may be several of them, each one specializing in a specific type of house plan and offering his service at some rate (service description). I need to choose one who fits my requirements (service discovery). Next, I need to contact a general contractor to build the house as per the plan. The general contractor has his own reliable plumbers, electricians, etc (service composition) and knows the timelines involved in bringing them in. In this case, I am the service consumer while the architects and contractors are the service providers. We need a framework (SOA) for matching needs and capabilities and for combining capabilities to address those needs. This requires that those with needs and those with capabilities are able to see each other (service discovery). This can be achieved by providing description of one's capability (service description) in a public or private forum (service advertisement).

Kailasam (2007) defined Service-oriented architecture as a "paradigm for organizing and utilizing distributed capabilities that may be under the control of different ownership domains" (p.2). In other words, this is a set of principles that defines a loosely coupled architecture and comprised of service providers and service consumers that interact according to a negotiated contract or interface. In terms of high level architecture, SOA consists of the following three components:

1. Service provider
2. Service registry
3. Service consumer

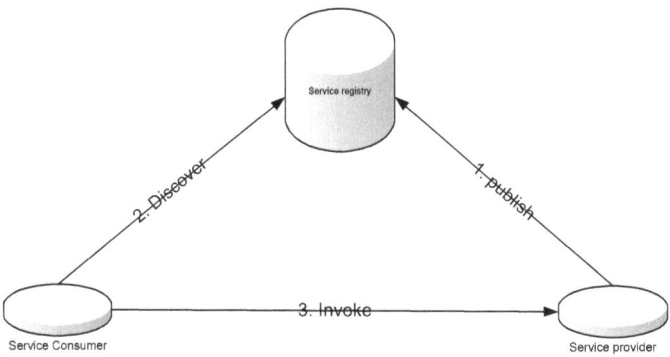

Figure1.1. Basic components of SOA

The service provider creates a service and publishes its interface and access information (service description) to a service registry. The registry is responsible for making the service interface and information about accessing implementation, available to service consumers. The service consumers locate (service discovery) entries in the service registry and binds to the service provider in order to invoke the defined service (service utilization). Each provider decides which of its services should be advertised, what sort of trading partner agreements are required to use the service and how to price the service. All these come under the service description banner. The implementers of the registry need to consider the implementation scope for the registry. For example, public service registries are available over the internet to an unrestricted audience while private service registries are accessible only to users within a company-wide intranet. Service discovery by consumers does not constitute automatic authorization to execute against the service.

The internet provides a uniform architecture of interaction between users and applications. For example, users interact well with applications on the web and they know what to expect. This is the power of a uniform and universal model as opposed to trying to develop hooks into new applications. Web service is a leading way of implementing SOA. It uses simple object access protocol (SOAP), an XML-based protocol over HTTP for communication between service providers and consumers. Services are advertised as interfaces defined by web service definition language (WSDL), whose semantics are defined in XML. Universal description discovery and integration (UDDI), a language independent protocol, is used for discovery of services and retrieval of their WSDL descriptions. Together, these standards allow disparate applications to discover and use the web services. Frameworks such as a Apache web service invocation frameworks (WSIF), allow applications to invoke web services without bothering about the details of service locations, data formats and protocols. The framework is able to figure out the details from WSDL at run-time and provide loosely coupled integration between service consumers and service providers.

III. Why businesses welcome this development

Today businesses are looking forward to reduced development time and faster time to market by reusing existing components across a wide range of projects. For this reason, businesses are jumping on the band wagon of service-oriented architecture development. Key business functionality is encapsulated into a service with well defined interface. Client invokes the service using the interface so that he is completely shielded from implementation details of the service because the services are built without any assumptions of who will consume these services. For example, let us say that user A works at company B and wants to check on a customer's order. This may require checking production status, inventory, and availability of parts. To collect that information, he may have to get access to a UNIX database as well as a mainframe in his own network, and go outside the company to get information from a supplier's web application. To get all that information (assuming he's using a Windows-based PC), he will have to switch between Windows and other applications and he has to know which applications to use and how to use them. Once he gathers the information, he will have to put them together manually, and then convey the details to the customer.

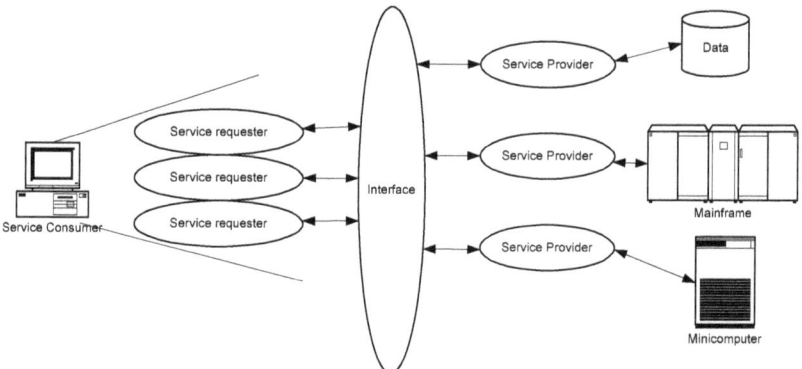

Figure1.2. Generic SOA infrastructure

The above diagram shows how user A could perform the same task through one interface if company B had adopted SOA. He needs the information from the same three sources, but that information is now collected behind a single interface in the SOA layer. Service requesters will invoke requests for the information by registering with the service registry, which sends the requests to the service providers. The service providers also register with the service registry so that it knows what services they provide. The service providers are the interfaces to the back-end business functions on the UNIX system, the mainframe and the supplier's web application. The information needed by user A is now collected automatically, so he no longer has to access each of the three functions directly and separately. A possible extension of SOA functionality is to eliminate user A and provide the details to the end customer directly. Avoiding duplications translates into real cost savings when changes need to be made.

Furthermore, SOA does not need to be fully implemented and deployed before benefits can accrue. As a matter of fact, SOA is ideally suited to incremental deployment where investment may be made on a step-by-step basis tied to individual business projects. Return on investment is also realized on an incremental basis thereby removing a major element of business risk in any justification process and greatly increasing the likelihood of acceptance by the business.

Chapter 2

I. Problem statement

As software implementation models change, the security assumptions and designs must be updated to manage the emerging threats, vulnerabilities and risks presented by the new way of doing business. SOA, by definition is loosely coupled, highly granular and often widely distributed and multi step. Unfortunately, the same "loose coupling" poses a challenge for anyone concerned with security and management at an enterprise level. The traditional application "siloed" approach to security and identity management for existing applications, where security functions such as authentication, authorization and audit were developed for each application silo leave security gaps within those organizations that have implemented SOA. The primary security mechanisms deployed today rely on notions of perimeter and centralized security models. As stated above, the nature of business is rapidly moving towards decentralized and intermingled process. At present, the perimeter security model does not apply to the service-oriented architecture. They are ineffective for companies already using this architecture, therefore threats and vulnerabilities left behind by the inadequate perimeter security model are being exploited. Security design assumptions based on outmoded technology create brittle and ineffective systems when deployed in a SOA environment. Traditional perimeter security model focuses on network security using one device to secure given assets. This was adequate as long as organizations do not allow customers to access the protected network and restrict them to the demilitarized zone. The diagram below shows a typical perimeter security view.

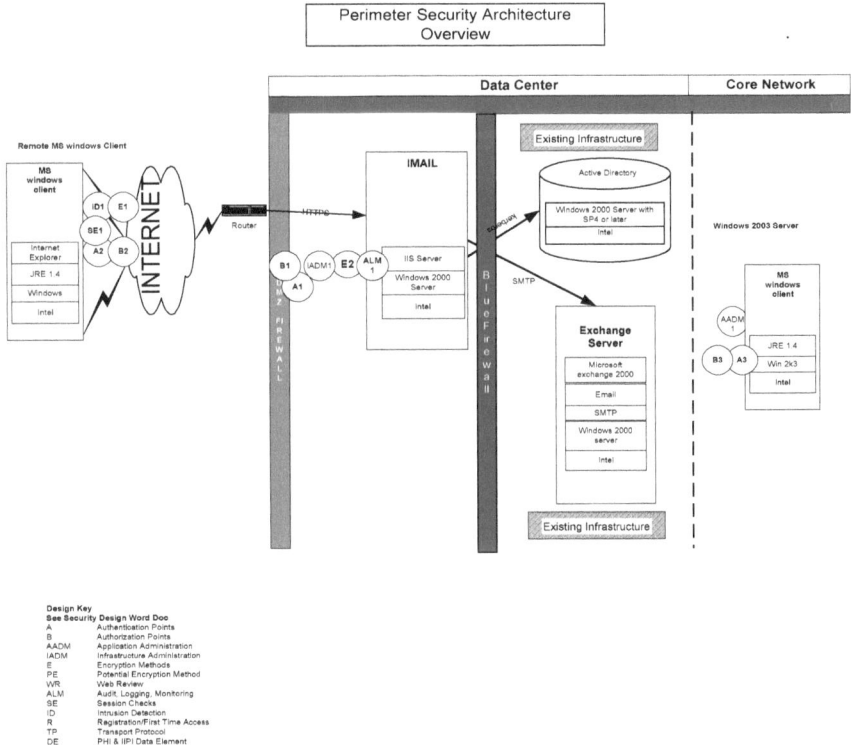

Figure 2.1. A traditional perimeter view of a security implementation.

The customers are always locked down to the external part of the network (DMZ). All resources have to be engineered in a way that requires authentication administration by the provider organization and the devices must also be accessible from inside the protected network. The data is always protected far away from the source which means that it is easy for data to transition from a secure to an insecure state between the source and the destination.

a) Existing Security model

Most organizations that have implemented SOA up to date are still using the perimeter concept of security. This concept is of the school of thought that there is a protected network and an unprotected network. The protected network is shielded from the unprotected part by perimeter devices, such as firewalls, border routers and intrusion detection systems. A demilitarized zone is created to serve customers that are not within the protected network. The DMZ contains servers that are exposed to the Internet and are used by the organization to fulfill business obligations. This concept believes that the borders of the network are static and protecting those static borders assures protection of those assets inside the borders. The perimeter security focuses on defense against OSI and TCP/IP model protocol vulnerabilities. The concept worked well for applications that are made just for resolving a specific business issue because the states of those applications were predictable based on the function.

b) Issues with using perimeter model to secure SOA

The primary method of corporate computer security over the past three decades has been focused around the network. It has been about allowing those inside the network to have privileged access to corporate resources and building impenetrable walls to keep outsiders out. Unfortunately, this model is rapidly loosing its effectiveness because the borders of networks are becoming much more fluid and dynamic with the advent of VPN, Web mail, and push e-mail on smart phones, telecommuters, and geographically dispersed and mobile workforce. The network boundaries are dissolving. There is not a clear distinction between safe and untrusted zones. The illusion of these categories, trusted/untrusted, safe/unsafe, is leading a lot of companies into believing a false sense of security. Once the organization takes a data-focused approach to security rather than a technology-focused approach, as soon as data is connected with interconnected computers via the internet, the perimeter fails.

Perimeter security mechanisms are not designed to handle the latest web service standards resulting in new avenues of attack for digital miscreants. A growing number of vendors are selling XML security gateways, appliances that can be plugged into a network and act as intermediary, decrypting and encrypting web service data to determine the authenticity and lock out attackers. SOA layouts expose applications by placing them just behind an outer layer of defense, rather than placing them within the inner walls of a company security defenses along with other critical applications and systems. Those applications are vulnerable because they are exposed to partners, customer relations management and supply chain management systems. Attackers can scan web service description language (the XML language used in web service calls) to find out where vulnerabilities lie. Perimeter security technologies are inadequate to protect SOA because they are dynamic and usually are not fully contained within the boundaries of a single network. Simple object access protocol (SOAP), which is also transmitted over HTTP is usually allowed through firewalls without restrictions. Transport layer security, which is used to authenticate and encrypt web based messages, is inadequate for SOAP messages because it is designed to operate only between two end points and cannot handle web services' ability to forward messages to multiple web services simultaneously. The web service processing model requires the ability to secure SOAP messages and XML documents as they are forwarded on long and complex chains of consumer, provider and intermediary services. These problems make the services subject to unique attacks in addition to variations on familiar attacks targeting web servers.

II. Solution

a) Architecture and Implementation requirements for SOA security

As stated above, the three building blocks for SOA implementation are service registration/deregistration, service discovery, and service invocation or delivery. In order to secure this architecture, there needs to be an understanding of the security requirement for each service.

Before service can be discovered and delivered, they must be registered in some repository. The repository may be external or residing in the same machine. In the latter case, stronger trust assumptions can be made while in the former, secure service registration is needed. The secure service registration means that authentication, authorization, integrity and confidentiality are maintained. Only authorized service providers must be allowed to register and deregister a service from the repository. Service must maintain its integrity while it is being registered and even after registration, and only the repository must receive the registered service. An attacker may eavesdrop on a registration message and replay it later, thus achieving some form of denial of service (DOS) attack. These issues should be considered during service registration.

If the discovery phase is compromised, then the consumer may end up invoking the malicious service. Security needs to ensure genuine discovery that is trustworthy. There is no point in having secure delivery with a phony service provider. Similar to service registration, security also need to ensure that only authorized users may use the discovery protocol, lest malicious users build an inventory of available services. Authorization may also be used to control the visibility of available services, for example, service description of certain services should only be retrieved at specific times. Security should also ensure confidentiality and integrity of the discovery messages; else attackers may get hold of the service list. If possible, security should seek to maintain anonymity of the users both in terms of identity and location.

Once the client has discovered the service, the next step is to invoke the service. However, in order to ensure that both the recipients as well as the service provider are genuine, mutual authentication needs to be performed. Confidentiality and integrity of the service needs to be ensured. Confidentiality ensures that only the intended recipient receives the services, while integrity proves that the message has not been modified in transit. Higher level services can be provided by composing together services in multiple security domains; hence standards need to be established for trust management across domains.

With the security architecture in place, the security implementation requirements should be the next focus. Approaching security requirements from a service-oriented architectural perspective raises some new requirements. These requirements address how to coordinate security mechanisms across business partners and trust boundaries and are defined in terms of policies in the following aspects:

1. When establishing trust between partners, the accurate definition of security policies covering transport, message, and data protection, including security tokens in a request, will be essential. In addition to having these policies, it is important to communicate these policies.
2. After a business has its own policies defined, it will need to manage and coordinate any changes of security information (signing or encryption keys) across partners.

In advance of interacting with a business partner's SOA resources, an organization need to determine appropriate security policies such as requirements for transport and message layer protection as well as data layer protection. These policies can provide a component of an overall assurance strategy leveraged by the individual businesses. They provide confidence that SOA will allow only authorized, trusted business partners with known and defined legal liability relationships, to participate in cross business transactions. In addition, the organization may need to implement such policies and monitor these implementations for business agreement and legal compliance.

Transport layer security refers to the type of protection offered in the actual delivery protocols involved in the interaction, such as secure socket layer (SSL) over internet transactions. SSL is used to provide confidential (encrypted) channel between two end points. The result of this encryption is that the contents of any message flowing over this channel are not discernable to any observing, outside party. This encryption is based on keys stored within digital SSL certificates. These are long-term keys bound to an entity during initial SSL session establishment. Both parties use a common new encryption key that is possibly previously unknown for the purposes of encrypting all of the messages on the wire. After SSL is terminated at the SSL end point, the messages are available in clear text for anyone to see (or alter). In a scenario where the SSL channel must be terminated and message forwarded to its intended destination service without using SSL (with intermediaries and gateways), there is a potential threat of exploit in the system. This leads us to the next requirement of message layer security.

Message layer security allows the system to protect the message body itself (transmitted in HTTP message body, for example) in terms of integrity and confidentiality. This is on top of any protection applied at the transport level. Since this is a message body security, the protection is end-to-end. Furthermore, transport layer security might change depending on the network boundaries that the message traverses (different levels of security over the many individual networks constituting the internet). End-to-end protection implies that the contents of the message cannot be read or modified at any point other than the required end point. In some cases, it is a requirement to protect both the message body and the headers. In general both message layer and transport layer security should be applied to messages within the SOA environments.

Data protection can be achieved with SOA by applying encryption mechanisms to the data-level elements within a message. Although not widely adopted, the notion of data element confidentiality is recognized as critical in many SOA implementations (especially those that will be applied within financial and health sector environments). Data element confidentiality enables individual data elements to be encrypted as opposed to encrypting an entire message. This element-level confidentiality allows protection of sensitive information (such as patient health information) while still allowing the exposure of other elements in a message for other purposes (such as coarse-grained authorization and routing).

At some level, cooperating business partners will determine the type of security tokens they can issue, manage, and exchange with each other. These tokens are used to assert information about requestors of business processes. As such, different scenarios require different tokens with various characteristics where appropriate. Some typical token types and their scenarios are as follows:

1. Username token: An identity assertion token that includes a password (usually in digest form). In general, web browsers and servers use this token in an HTTP environment in which the intelligent browser collects a username and password that is then validated by the service provider. A special form of a username token is an IDAssertion. This is a username

token without password, generally used within a trusted environment in which the security token is used to communicate or assert an already authenticated identity.

2. X.509 certificate: This is typically used to identify a requestor that has signed part or all of a message. The certificate provides a "two-for-one" approach for identifying the requestor based on information already included in the request by the requestor.

3. Security assertion markup language (SAML) assertion: This provides a means of asserting an identity or providing attributes for a claimed identity. A SAML assertion is typically used in a passive client scenario (for single sign-on) or in an active client scenario when additional information about a requestor is required (such as attributes describing the user's roles, groups, and privileges).

4. Kerberos token: It is based on an authentication mechanism designed at MIT and since adopted by Microsoft as a means of asserting identity.

An SOA environment requires that partners establish key management policies when used for signing or encrypting information. This is both a security consideration and a legal one. Security speaking, one should never use the same key pair for both signing and encryption. SSL certificates are easy to come by, businesses running large volumes of high-dollar transactions will almost certainly require more assurance of their business partner's identity than a free or self-generated SSL certificate.

Establishing common policies for transport layer security across the enterprise is a well understood exercise today. Almost all businesses using the internet have SSL certificates. Businesses have good procedures in place for managing such certificates and SSL sessions with the help of IETF-defined standards. However, other aspects of SOA security requirements discussed earlier are less understood. As business process become service oriented, organizations can no longer assume messages will be bound to just the well known HTTP transport layer. When considering web service requests, companies need to leverage well-defined message structures based on XML and SOAP with their respective security mechanisms. XML encryption, XML digital signature, and the WS-Security road map describe the mechanisms necessary for any security strategy for service-oriented architectures. Therefore, for organizations to understand how to define and relate policies to transactions that span between companies, it is necessary to look at the mechanisms and protocol that allows it.

b) Service-Oriented Security architecture overview

In software architecture, the word "security" can often do more harm than good. Frequently stakeholders have differing, conflicting and overloaded definition of the term. In order to build a coherent system, architects must provide a specific guidance to the development and operational teams. As stated by Peterson (2005), "Service-oriented security and its architectural view provide a framework for reasoning about software security in a service oriented system" (p.326). It provides a set of software architecture view point that allows security architects to construct a holistic system design based on a set of views. No single view is sufficient to analyze and understand the system's security as a whole. The combinations of service-oriented security views and their relationships demonstrate the security decisions and design. Since security is not a zero sum game, the views provide a framework in which to conduct security architecture tradeoff analysis and to convey design decisions to development and operational staff. The views enable the software architect to separate concerns in a complex system.

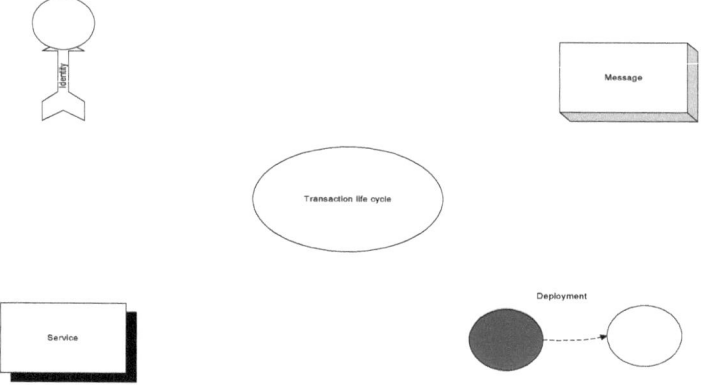

Figure2.2. Systems and business security architecture (SABSA) Service-

oriented security views

The identity view deals with the generation, communication, recognition and transformation of identity. The service view deals with the service, its methods and component parts. The message view focuses on the service's message payload. The deployment view deals with the defense-in-depth five layer model: physical, network, host, application and data. The transaction life cycle view is concerned with key behavioral flows and relationships in a system and its actors from end-to-end perspective.

Each of these views is composed of domain specific elements, constraints, threats, risks, vulnerabilities and countermeasures. Each view also includes a set of key architectural patterns and principles. By partitioning concerns, security designers are able to decouple domain concerns and analyze tradeoffs and dependencies among the domain. The resultant architecture takes the concerns from each domain into account and provides holistic solutions based on the risk management of digital assets like identities and data.

c) Service-oriented Security views

Software security architecture is an iterative process that includes decomposing complex problem spaces, drilling down on granular details to gain traction in a domain; and then synthesizing across domains, building up design views, identifying relationship vectors that illustrate the system's security design goals. Each service-oriented security view contains the following constituents:

1. Elements: describes the key components in the system and their logical organization including the subject and objects that the view interacts with.
2. Constraints: shows the business, political, legal and technical constraints for the view
3. Risk model: illustrates the threats, assets, vulnerabilities and countermeasures in the view.
4. Relationships: conveys the nature and direction of the views' relationships with other views.

The chief utility of separation of concerns in the service-oriented security is that each of the views' elements, constraints, risk models, and relationships are unique and decoupled inside their view. The design decision made about securing the elements will impact other views, but separating the concerns allows for decoupling the concerns and handling the domain specific risks.

The identity view examines identity as a set of claims made by one digital subject about itself or another. This definition reveals that identity is not a passive entity, but rather the result of an active set of processes that can be judged against a dynamic set of criteria. When identity is defined as a set of claims, each service can decide what claims it will accept and from what authorities. The key elements of identity view include authentication mechanisms, events, and principals including Kerberos tickets, X.509, Windows sessions, and web server sessions. The second element is the identity federation including the portable, strong identities like SAML, Liberty and WS-federation identities. Monitoring and audit systems also have to be in place to provide traceability of identity related events. Identity is a fundamental element in access control decisions; hence the protocol that generates, communicate and negotiate identity information requires security analysis to ensure a robust system. Identity information is a very valuable asset to attackers and so system designers must design its implementation and usage to withstand a variety of attacks. Phishing attacks that continue to grow in distribution and sophistication are just one example of attacks that exploit weak identity system. Privacy, regulatory and legal domains all impose constraints on identity implementation and what information may be shared and used by parties. Identity information may leak inadvertently to other systems and users that are not allowed to access the information.

A typical scenario of an identity view pattern using federated identity can help clarify the use of the elements mentioned above.

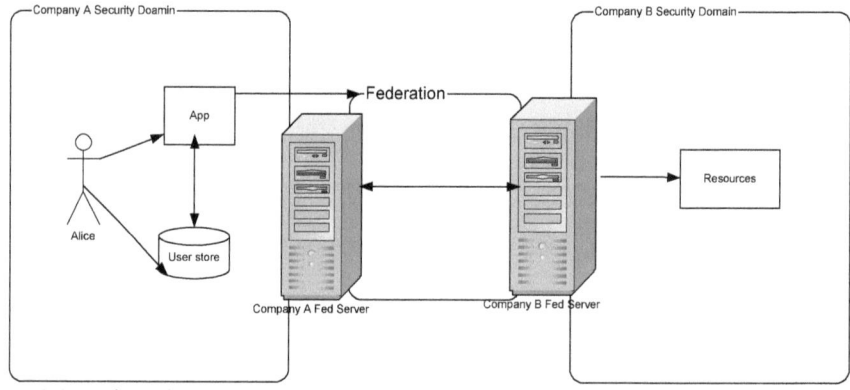

Figure2.3. Using Identity Federation

Assume company A and company B wants to integrate disparate systems with unique policies and management. The systems have disparate identity repositories, operating systems, and application languages, but want to exchange XML documents for order processing. User credentials must be securely ported across domains and security information must be recognizable to both parties. Using federated identity, company A client (Alice) logs onto local company A system, generates/sends encrypted SAML token with app request to company B server (service provider). Company B server validates assertions for access rights. This is one of many implementation of the identity view. The view has relationships with the other service-oriented security views. It provides information about subjects to the other views, while other views both consume and query principal data provided by the processes generated by identity view elements. Due to its criticality as the foundation element for other views, it should be hardened using the strongest security controls that are reasonably possible for all the states of the system that the identity is in.

The service view provides the interface to the rest of the system and brokers the identity, messages and transactional data. It is concerned with the risks around the service and the service's ability to broker information flows with the required confidentiality, integrity and availability. Services require access control protection and may consume identity and domain attribute information from other domains. From a detection and response standpoint, services require logging mechanisms to vouch for the health of the system. Standard technology specific service hardening and security guidelines apply in the service view such as open web application security project (OWASP) guidelines for web applications. Key elements of service view include application servers and services, such as databases, web servers and services, logging services and integrity services. The concerned risks for this view include denial of service, forcing exception conditions, attacks against validation systems, attacks against program and service logic. Since services are an endpoint for incoming requests, they must broker access and data flows between the domains with disparate security models. The use of security pipeline interface (SPI) to enforce the principle of separation of privilege will reduce risk of data integrity threats.

Information security is concerned with protecting valuable digital assets, in many cases most valuable assets from a risk management perspective is not network access, but company data. As distributed systems continue to evolve and become more connected to each other in ways not foreseen by their original designers, such as decades old legacy systems being connected to the web, data and messages emerge in ways not intended when their protection mechanisms were implemented. The result is to move security mechanisms closer to the asset level, in this case, data elements. Encryption and related technology standards are used to constrain access to persistent data while it is at rest and ensure integrity and audit ability over its life cycle. The key elements in the message view are message payload, typically XML documents and related schema information, interface information like WSDL in web services and security tokens such as digital signature information and cryptographic keys. Security risks that may plague the message view include attacks against data at rest and in transit. Since data flows in service oriented systems cannot be predicted in an end to end sense with any high degree of confidence, encryption is a primary consideration for protecting messages as it traverses different domains. Most implementation of SOA uses the WS-security standard to sign and encrypt persistent XML documents. It uses XML encryption and XML signature and can accept tokens such as SAML, Kerberos, and X.509 to provide assurance through authentication, authorization and validation.

The deployment environment view is focused on classic information security defense-in-depth layers such as physical, network, host, application and data. This is where the lion share of IT resources is currently deployed. The patterns are so more matured than those in the emerging SOA-centric views previously discussed. The risks present in the defense-in-depth layer must be base lined against the SOA applications that are deployed on these foundations.

The transaction life cycle view shows the end-to-end view of the system. Use case provides a synthetic model that correlates requirements from different domains' concerns into a coherent model and flow. Use case models contain many properties that are critical to secure system design:

1. Stakeholders- In information security, it pays to find allies who have vested interest in system security
2. Pre and post conditions that must be satisfied for use case to execute and the set of states that the system can be in after it has completed
3. Exceptional and alternate flows that highlight paths that often become attack vectors. These flows are worth examination to ensure that the system is designed to deal with the exceptions and has deployed security mechanisms such as audit logs, intrusion detection tools to catch security exceptions when they occur.
4. Actors are computer systems, users and schedulers. By analyzing the

actors involved in the use case model, the information security team can begin to build a picture of the access control structures such as roles and groups that may be required for design as the system is built.

5. Mapping use cases to threat models- Security must always consider the attacker's viewpoint. Threat modeling is always used in the development life cycle to map possible threats, vulnerabilities and impacts onto the system so that appropriate security countermeasures can be built into the system.

        d) Service-Oriented security models, standards and mechanisms

A reference model is an abstract framework for understanding significant relationships among the entities of an environment. Reference model consists of a minimal set of unifying concepts, axioms and relationships within a particular problem domain. It is independent of specific standards, technologies or implementations. It enables the development of concrete architecture. The SOA reference model has three components: base security services, security policy infrastructure and business security services.

Base security services are building blocks to provide the basic security services. These services can be used like a black box by different components in the SOA environment, like service consumers, service providers, proxy servers and application servers. They provide the basic security functions like confidentiality, authentication, authorization, audit and non-repudiation.

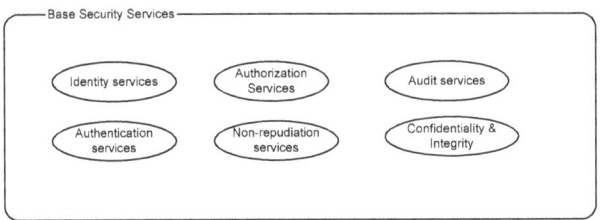

Figure2.4. Base security service reference model

In the context of SOA, policies are used to specify the behavior of the underlying infrastructure as well as express the conditions to be satisfied by consumers for accessing them. When a service is created and stored in the service registry, the security policy infrastructure receives the service definitions and the meta-data. It then defines the security policy based on them. Once the policies are defined, they are distributed in a common format (WS-Policy) to the enforcement points.

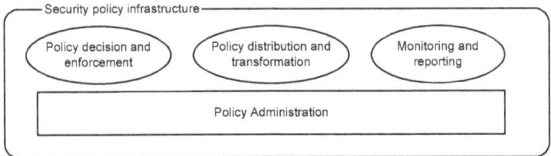

Figure2.5. Security policy reference model

It is necessary to provide a secure deployment environment where business solutions can be deployed and hosted. Since SOA solutions can extend across multiple organizations, it is necessary for the participating organization to achieve a common set of standards for communication across enterprise boundaries. Similarly, at the top level, trust policies need to be agreed upon by participating entities. Business policies need to be defined to control access to sensitive data, and processes need to be in place to penalize violation of policies. SOA security reference model acts as a checklist for implementing security requirements. A typical deployment scenario is illustrated below:

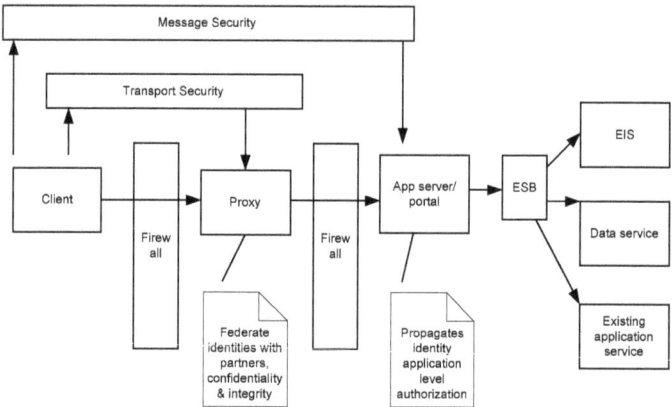

Figure2.6. Security deployment scenario for SOA

Standards have special relevance to SOA security implementation, primarily web services, as they form the crucial backbone for implementation security solutions. A plethora of security standards are being worked on at different standard bodies to enable faster adoption of services and grid technologies. Some of those standards are basic security standards, message level and element level encryption, trust domains, federated security, session management, authorization and policies.

The basic security standard is the WS-security published by Microsoft, IBM and Verisign. The specification was originally published in April 2002 by IBM, Microsoft and Verisign and subsequently was submitted to the OASIS web services security technical committee (WSS-TC). The effort through the OASIS process led to an OASIS standard in March 2004 known as web service security. The specification provides three main mechanisms: sending security tokens as part of a message, message integrity and message confidentiality. WS-Security enables the application of XML security techniques to authenticate and secure message exchanges between service requestor and a service provider. It uses signature and encryption placed on a message and security tokens bound to the messages. The WS-Security specification is agnostic to the type of token that is actually included within a message. It uses an XML approach to define tokens that enables extensibility and supports multiple security tokens. The digital signature, used to ensure confidentiality and integrity in service interactions, can be implemented with XML digital signature (XML-DSig). XML-DSig was a joint initiative of the internet engineering task force (IETF) and the World Wide Web consortium (W3C).

XML encryption is a W3C recommendation that is not just a means of encrypting XML but also to express meta-information about the encryption performed on a digital document. This allows the document processor to be aware of what algorithms were used to encrypt the document.

The web service trust specification (WS-Trust) defines a mechanism for issuing and exchanging security tokens between partners. Token exchange provides the means of issuing and disseminating credentials within and across different trust domains. It provides tokens for use in WS-Security message exchanges and uses the mechanism within the WS-Security to ensure its own messages.

WS-Federation specification describes how to use the existing web services security building blocks that allows business processes to work in federated groups. It focuses on the relationships between parties and the high-level architecture that supports these relationships. Two additional documents, WS-Federation active and WS-Federation passive profile specification, describes how to implement individual federation solutions. WS-Federation allows an active client application entity to include the required information to identify the requestor and its privileges within its request. This allows the authentication and authorization of request in an implied browser-based HTTP-based environment, to be replicated in a SOA environment without browser or direct user interaction.

The WS-SecureConversation specification describes how to leverage WS-Security and WS-Trust to authenticate a series of messages within a conversation, hence establishing a secure conversation. A secure conversation is managed by a security context, represented by a security context token (SCT). This token contains a shared secret (symmetric key) that is in turn, used to manage the secure conversation. The secret key can be used to sign messages that belong to a particular conversation. The specification recommends that this SCT be used as part of an additional negotiation to establish a derived key used to sign and encrypt messages, for a set of messages associated with this security context.

The WS-Policy specification implies three core specifications: WS-Policy framework, WS-PolicyAttachments, and WS-PolicyAssertions. The policy framework defines a general purpose model and corresponding syntax to describe and communicate web services policies that service consumers need to know to be able to access services from a service provider. The framework provides flexible and extensible grammar for expressing the capabilities, requirement and general characteristics of entities in an XML web services-based system. The WS-PolicyAttachments specification defines how policies are associated with web service artifacts like WSDL, UDDI, and endpoint references for deployed web services.

e) Service-oriented security management

After the implementation of a secure SOA solution, the organization needs to be able to manage the security infrastructure, including managing trust relationship, security tokens for authentication, security tokens for session management, and credential stores.

Trust relationships are usually derived from the use of cryptographic techniques such as public key infrastructure. Simply having and exchanging cryptographic elements across business partners is not sufficient to establish and maintain a trust relationship. Part of a trust relationship also involves asserting and accepting requestor identities and attributes across the established trust relationships. For this reason, it is integral to manage the tokens used to convey this information.

Services can use X.509 certificates as the basis for security tokens to convey authentication information to sign a message. A trust service's security token functionality validates security tokens to authenticate requestors.

The WS-SecureConversation specification is an extension of the WS-Trust credential acquisition model that describes how to request and use a secure conversation token for long running conversations and sessions. The SCT provides the logical equivalent of SSL session management in an HTTP transport bound environment. A trust service security token should create and validate SCT.

In addition to trust service management, trust services (or more specifically, logical security token service) can also act as credential stores. In many environments information about requestor is propagated throughout the environment for many different purposes (for example, audit, logging, and request authorization). Rather than carrying a large credential around with each request, it is easier to carry a credential reference. This credential reference can then be used by the security token service to appropriately look up the actual credentials when required during request processing.

f) Service-Oriented security Architecture issues

The service-oriented security views describe a way of seeing security architecture across a complex system to make and convey security design decisions. The software security space contains issues that are still being worked to achieve optimal effectiveness.

Research has shown various flaws with XML security related to its reliance on XML for encryption and signatures as well as replicating a number of problems in legacy technologies. Since a larger number of emerging security solutions, particularly WS-* rely on XML security mechanisms, it is worth revisiting this dependency to see if extensible messaging and presence protocol (XMPP) or other technology can remedy the issues.

The software security space is evolving at a rapid pace; investment paths are not clear in a long term sense. Deploying resources based on today's assumptions about standards, implementation and threat models inserts a higher degree of variability into the system's longevity based on the outcomes of the technical and standard challenges.

As with any security design, the opponent is ever adaptable and resourceful. As security designs become more robust, businesses deploy more resources and transactions to the online world, thus attracting more attackers.

Chapter 3

I. How the research contributes to the security industry body of knowledge

This book provides an opportunity and motivation for taking another look at the security mechanisms currently deployed in a business in support of a set of business services. It is an opportunity to look at encapsulating or decomposing complex security mechanisms into a set of related security services. This book did that by identifying the points at which security decisions are made and those points where they can be enforced. The book challenged the reader to think about security as a service within SOA by focusing on security as an infrastructure service in the context of an enterprise service bus.

II. Future trends in SOA security

Today SOA is being embraced by enterprises for its loosely-coupled nature. Due to this, security has become a major concern. This paper looked at the basic security implementation in SOA environment. This paper showed that the current use of SSL/TLS is not enough to ensure SOA security. Technology standards have emerged to enhance SOA security. Now that these standards are in place, it is necessary to ensure interoperability between the different concrete implementations of these standards. A seamless secure user experience would be the future goal. It would be nice to provide reliable messaging as a service (it should be possible to assert the QOS required) whether any transaction support is needed and the system should work.

Chapter 4

The basic principles of applying security in any software solution are about identifying the risks, evaluating them, and then formulating a plan to mitigate them. In SOA-based systems, these security principles are the same. However, additional factors are introduced because SOA proposes distributed services and decoupled application systems. To effectively secure these resources, a gamut of technology options and variations are available with accompanying performance and operational management overheads. Mapping the security risks to the solution options requires careful planning and should be conducted formally during inception of an SOA endeavor. Still the ability of businesses to trust this technology will not be based on generic technology alone. To bootstrap into trusting technology for delegating trust, business must first trust strategic vendors and partners to apply such technology to specific business relationships. These vendors will be trusted only when they have earned that trust by repeatedly delivering successful business solutions. Part of this trust should be based on the vendors' mastery of diverse technologies to be federated by the service-oriented security architecture and its competence and capabilities in deploying, managing, and auditing such technologies.

References

Bierberstein, N. (2006). *Service-Oriented Architecture Compass: Business value, planning, and enterprise roadmap.* Upper saddle river, NJ: IBM press.

Capgemini Government Solution LLC. (2007, 12/06). *Service-Oriented Security Architecture and Deperimeterization.*, Capgemini, Herndon, VA.

Gossels, J., & Mackey. Jr., R. (2005, 01/12). Service Oriented Architecture:Security Challenges. In *0.08* (Leadership in Security and Compliance). Retrieved 08312007, from www.systemexperts.com.

Hassan, J. (2004). *Expert Service-Oriented Architecture in C#-Using the Web Services Enhancement 2.0.* Germany: Apress.

Hinton, H., Honodo, M., & Hutchison, B. (2005, November). Service-Oriented Architecture. In *8* (Security Patterns Within a Service-Oriented Architecture). Retrieved 09012007, from IBM: http://www.ibm.com/websphere/developer/services.

Johnston, S. (2004, 24/06). Modeling Security Concerns in Service-Oriented Architectures. In *10*. Retrieved 09012007, from IBM: http://www-128.ibm.com/developerworks/rational/library/4860.html.

Kailasam, S. (2007, 12/August). *Security Challenges in Service Oriented Architecture.* Term Paper, Computer Science and Engineering, Madras, India.

Kall, N. (2003, 27/10). Service-Oriented Security Architecure. In *0.10* (Techupdate). Retrieved 31072007, from Zdnet: http://techupdate.zdnet.com/techupdate/stories/main/Service_Oriented_Security_Architecture.

Padmanabhuni, S. (2006). *Security in Service-Oriented Architecture-Issues, Standards and Implementations.* Software Engineering and Technology labs, Infosys Technologies Limited, India.

Peterson, G. (2005, November). Security Architecture. *Information Security*

Bulletin, 10(0), 325-326.

Willet, K. (2007, 2/01). Security Issues in Service-Oriented Architecture. In *0.09* (CSC World Featured Article). Retrieved 02052007, from CSC hosting service: http://www.csc.com/cscworld/012007/fa/fa005.shtml.

www.ingramcontent.com/pod-product-compliance
Ingram Content Group UK Ltd.
Pitfield, Milton Keynes, MK11 3LW, UK
UKHW041433180426
11947UKWH00007B/414